D0772249

let's celebrate

valentine's day

by J. Patrick Lewis

Children's Press®
An Imprint of Scholastic Inc.

Library of Congress Cataloging-in-Publication Data
A CIP catalog record for this book is available from the Library of Congress

Produced by Spooky Cheetah Press
Design by Anna Tunick Tabachnik (www.atunick.com)
Fonts: Coco Gothic, ITC Stone Informal
Clouds by freepik.com
Special thanks to Pamela Chanko for editorial advice

© 2018 by Scholastic Inc.
All rights reserved. Published in 2018 by Children's Press, an imprint of Scholastic Inc.

Printed in Heshan, China 62

SCHOLASTIC, CHILDREN'S PRESS, ROOKIE POETRY™, and associated logos are trademarks and/or registered trademarks of Scholastic Inc.

1 2 3 4 5 6 7 8 9 10 R 27 26 25 24 23 22 21 20 19 18

Photos ©: cover main: LilKar/Shutterstock; cover left: Niday Picture Library/Alamy Images; cover right: Sheri Blaney/Getty Images; cover grass: Sailorr/Shutterstock; back cover bottom: Niday Picture Library/Alamy Images; back cover top and throughout: jannoon028/Shutterstock; 1: prapann/Shutterstock; 2-3: invictus999/ iStockphoto; 4: Niday Picture Library/Alamy Images; 5: Choreograph/Getty Images; 5 top left and throughout: Sheri Blaney/Getty Images; 6-7 top: 5 second Studio/Shutterstock; 6 bottom right: Circa/Getty Images; 7 background: ESOlex/Shutterstock; 7 center: Sawitree Pamee/EyeEm/Getty Images; 7 bouquet: Murina Natalia/ Shutterstock; 8-9 pink petals: Anelina/Shutterstock; 8-9 red petals: Picsfive/Shutterstock; 9 border: Edyta Linek/ Dreamstime; 9 rose: Damedeeso/Dreamstime; 9 dog: Javier Brosch/Shutterstock; 10 top: IllustratedHistory/ Alamy Images; 10 bottom: The Granger Collection; 11 main: nautilus_shell_studios/iStockphoto; 11 left heart: nkbimages/iStockphoto; 11 center heart: Deborah Dixon/Dreamstime; 11 right: IllustratedHistory/Alamy Images; 12 top: Andreka/Getty Images; 12 bottom: IllustratedHistory/Alamy Images; 13 main: Stephanie Rausser/Getty Images; 13 flowers: Khunaspix/Dreamstime; 14 top candy and throughout: ale de sun/Shutterstock; 14 cupids: swim ink 2 llc/ Getty Images; 14 cupcake: 578foot/Getty Images; 14 lollipops and throughout: Yuriyzhuravov/Dreamstime; 14 chocolate and throughout: Sabina Pensek/Dreamstime; 14 top hearts and throughout: Oleksandr Voloshyn/Dreamstime; 15 top left candy and throughout: Sparkia/Dreamstime; 15 center: Paper Boat Creative/Getty Images; 15 macaroons: Daria Saveleva/ Shutterstock; 15 hand: Phonix_a Pk.sarote/Shutterstock; 15 cookies: nata_vkusidey/Getty Images; 16 cat: ZCHE/izzyandthefluff/ WENN/Newscom; 16 penguin: Sue Flood/Getty Images; 16-17 balloons: Andreka/iStockphoto; 17 cow: Sebastian Knight/Shutterstock; 17 swans: John Crabb/Alamy Images; 18 bottom: Circa/age fotostock; 18 top and throughout: Gregor Schuster/Getty Images; 18-19 background: kevron2001/Getty Images; 19 kid silos: Nazarenko LLC/Shutterstock; 19 butterfly and throughout: Circa/Getty Images; 20 top left: The Photolibrary Wales/Alamy Images; 20 top center: The Photolibrary Wales/Alamy Images; 20 top right: Budimir Jevtic/ Shutterstock; 21 bottom left: Kyodo/AP Images; 21 top: Alessandro Cristiano/Shutterstock; 21 bottom right: Glow Images, Inc/Getty Images; 22 top right: IllustratedHistory/Alamy Images; 23 center: Blue_Cutler/Getty Images; 23 center bottom: Anelina/Shutterstock; top: Stephanie Rausser/Getty Images; 23 bottom: Circa/Getty Images; 23 center top: IllustratedHistory/Alamy Images;

table of contents

happy valentine's day!

On Valentine's Day, I wonder why
heart-shaped balloons
 fill up the sky.
I think it's so the world can see
how beautiful a heart can be.

4

FACT! In the U.S., half of all adults celebrate Valentine's Day.

gifts for everyone

Who do you love on Valentine's Day?
Your cat, your dog, your mother?
Give them a **treat** to show
  how much...
Oops! Don't forget your brother!

FACT! Jewelry is the **most** popular Valentine's gift.

love in bloom

I'm your puppy, I'm your prince
of valentines—these flowers
are a **rosy** red **reminder**:
You can tickle me for hours!

FACT! In the U.S., 250 million roses are grown for Valentine's Day.

from me to you

When Teacher said, "What can you do
with paper hearts, crayons, and glue?"
I made this card,
it wasn't hard,
because I made it just for you!

I LOVE YOU DADDY!

Happy Valentine's Day!

FACT! In the U.S., about 190 million Valentine cards are exchanged yearly.

For you

13

kiss me once

Kiss me once, kiss me twice,
wouldn't that be **grand**?
Still it's almost just as nice
blowing kisses hand to hand.

FACT! Chocolate kisses are the 2nd most popular Valentine's candy.

the sweetest thing

I'll give you a chocolate lollipop,
I'll give you a red-hot heart,
but if you will be my valentine,
that's the sweetest part!

REAL LOVE

SURE LOVE

LOVE YOU

IT'S LOVE

FACT! The No. 1 Valentine's candy is chocolate in a heart-shaped box.

lovebirds

Flamingos can kiss,
that's a **peck** on the beak.
Two wings for a hug—
that's a cuddle
cheek to cheek!

FACT! Lovebirds like to cuddle—just like people do!

love,
the tree of life

I've never seen a tree
as beautiful as this.
It is as if Mother Nature
is giving the Earth a kiss.

To my Valentine

With Smile Divine I greet you My Valentine To keep you

FACT! Teachers get the most Valentine's cards!

love celebrations around the world

United Kingdom

A spoonful of love
In Wales, a person may give a lovespoon to his or her valentine. This wooden spoon is hand-carved with special symbols, like hearts, keys, and flowers.

Germany

A visit from Father Valentine In Norfolk, Jack Valentine comes to visit on this lovely holiday. Also known as Old Father Valentine, he leaves gifts and candy for children and adults.

I love you. Here's a pig! In Germany, a pig is the symbol of Valentine's Day! People may exchange piggy pictures and figurines. They even give each other chocolate pigs.

20

Japan

My turn, your turn
In Japan, women give gifts on Valentine's Day. The next month, men give gifts to their valentines.

South Africa

Guess who loves you
On February 14, women in South Africa write the name of someone they love on a heart. Then they pin the heart on a sleeve of their shirt for all to see.

Argentina

All week long
In Argentina, people exchange candy for seven days during Sweetness Week, which usually ends with a Friendship Day.

valentines day is...

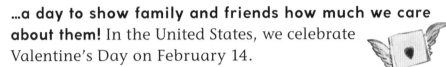

...a day to show family and friends how much we care about them! In the United States, we celebrate Valentine's Day on February 14.

Almost 2,000 years ago, the emperor of Rome made it illegal to get married. He wanted young men to become soldiers. He did not want them settling down to family life. A priest named Valentine thought this was unfair. He helped people wed secretly. For this, Valentine was put in jail and killed. He was later made a saint. And Saint Valentine's Day became a time to celebrate all the people we love.

It is fun to celebrate Valentine's Day. We have parties. We decorate paper hearts. We give cards and candy to our friends. People also give flowers to the people they love or buy or make them small gifts. Valentine's Day is a great time to say, "I love you!"

glossary

grand (GRAND): Something that is wonderful or very enjoyable.

peck (PEK): A quick, light kiss.

reminder (ri-MINE-dur): Something that helps a person remember.

rosy (ROH-zee): Having a pinkish color.

treat (TREET): Something special, like a surprise or a gift.

index

facts for now

Visit this Scholastic Web site to learn more about Valentine's Day:
www.factsfornow.scholastic.com Enter the keyword **Valentine**

about the author

J. Patrick Lewis has published 100 children's picture and poetry books to date with a wide variety of publishers. The Poetry Foundation named him the third U.S. Children's Poet Laureate.